CLASSIC DIESEL YEARS
NORTHUMBERLAND

PAUL SHANNON

No. 37069 passes Freeman's crossing on the Cambois Branch with empty air-braked hoppers from Blyth power sation on 21 June 1982.

© Paul Shannon, 2024
First published in the United Kingdom, 2024,
by Stenlake Publishing Ltd.
54-58 Mill Square, Catrine, KA5 6RD
www.stenlake.co.uk
ISBN 978-1-84033-977-2

The publishers regret that they cannot supply copies of any pictures featured in this book.

Printed by
P2D Books, 1 Newlands Rd, Westoning, Bedford MK45 5LD

No. 56080 prepares to depart from Ashington with air-braked hoppers on 17 July 1986.

Introduction

This album takes readers on a nostalgic tour of railways in the historic county of Northumberland – and some neighbouring areas of County Durham and Cumberland where it made sense to include them – focusing mainly on the 1980s when first-generation diesels were still firmly in charge of everyday passenger and freight operations.

In 1980, Northumberland was served by two long-distance rail routes – the East Coast Main Line running from south to north and the Tyne Valley Line running from east to west. The one-time suburban network on the north side of the Tyne – essentially a circular route from Newcastle to the coast via South Gosforth and back via Wallsend – was undergoing conversion to Metro operation, eventually leaving BR with only a limited local service on the East Coast Main Line to Morpeth and Alnmouth.

Many East Coast expresses were in the hands of High Speed Train (later InterCity 125) sets, but the last of the Class 55 Deltics hung on until the end of 1981 Around that time some trains were still hauled by other types such as Classes 40, 46 and 47. Electric traction became the norm in 1991. Local trains in Northumberland were almost exclusively formed of Metropolitan-Cammell Class 101 DMUs, although limited locomotive haulage extended along the Tyne Valley Line including some latter-day forays by Deltics. The first two-axle Pacer units entered service in the mid-1980s, followed by other second-generation diesel units.

Northumberland's freight traffic in the early 1980s was still dominated by coal. About ten collieries and opencast sites in the county dispatched coal by rail, and local destinations included Blyth power sation, Stella North and South power stations and the historic staiths at West Blyth, as well as residual traffic to coal depots such as Haltwhistle and Morpeth. The extensive National Coal Board operation at Ashington remarkably survived until 1986. It was coal traffic that ensured the survival of large sections of the Blyth and Tyne network, which had lost its regular passenger services in 1964.

Aside from coal, several freight-only branch lines survived into the 1980s including the rump of the Riverside Branch to Carville, the branch partly over Tyne and Wear Metro tracks to Coxlodge and Callerton, and the furthest section of the Cambois Branch to North Blyth alumina terminal.

Freight haulage in the diesel era was traditionally dominated by Class 37s, but several other types appeared as well, especially on the main lines. These pages show examples of Classes 31, 40, 47 and 27 on freight duties, as well as ex-BR Class 14s at Ashington and the new Class 56s which were becoming established on air-braked coal trains.

The variety of classic diesel traction is complemented by railway settings which in some cases had changed little since the 19th century. Mechanical signal boxes still controlled most of the Tyne Valley and Blyth and Tyne networks in the 1980s, with some particularly fine examples of overhead boxes at Hexham and Wylam. Remarkably, the Tyne Valley Line is still largely manually signalled today, while the Blyth and Tyne system has only recently lost some of its North Eastern Railway boxes as preparations are made for a restored passenger service.

No. 55015 *Tulyar* passes Brampton Fell with the return working of the 'Hadrian Flyer' railtour from Carlisle to Peterborough on 5 December 1981.

Facing page: No. 37106 bypasses the platforms of Newcastle Station with a train of unfitted 21-ton and 24½-ton coal hopper wagons on 26 July 1979, likely to have been en route from one of the Durham collieries to Blyth for shipment. At that time there were still four goods lines on the south side of the station, but freight traffic was in decline and these lines were occupying space that could better be used for passenger services. BR therefore remodelled the track layout in the late 1980s with a new island platform straddling the southern wall. The photograph also shows one of the Class 03 shunters which were once common on station pilot duties, as well as a Cravens DMU and No. 40083 on a northbound passenger service.

The first railway crossing between Gateshead and Newcastle was the six-span, two-tier High Level Bridge, designed by Robert Stephenson and completed in 1849. This structure played a key role in the development of the East Coast Main Line, with through trains between London and Edinburgh becoming possible once an even bigger structure – the Royal Border Bridge across the Tweed – opened in the following year. With its original three-track layout still intact, a pair of Metropolitan-Cammell Class 101 units crosses the High Level Bridge on a service from the Durham Coast on 13 September 1980. The three tracks on the bridge were reduced to two in the late 1980s, while the road deck hidden beneath the railway now comprises a single southbound carriageway for buses and taxis and footpaths for pedestrians and cyclists.

Facing page: Deltic No. 55008 *The Green Howards* rolls into Newcastle Station after crossing the King Edward Bridge with the 05.50 from London Kings Cross to Aberdeen on 8 December 1981. The four-track King Edward Bridge opened in 1906 and enabled London-Edinburgh trains to avoid reversing at Newcastle. The tracks curving to the right formed the original passenger line from the Tyne Valley via Scotswood, closed as a through route in 1982. No. 55008 was near the end of its life when this photograph was taken: it failed with flat batteries at Finsbury Park on 31 December and was withdrawn after 7,842 days in service. Only one of its cabs survived the cutter's torch.

The complex layout of points and crossings at the east end of Newcastle Station was once considered one of the wonders of the railway world, especially after it was relaid in 1912 using manganese castings. The diamond crossings were necessary in order to give trains from South Shields and the Durham Coast access to the bay platforms on the north side of the station. The layout was simplified in the late 1970s but still provided the photographer with an impressive view from the Castle Keep on 13 September 1980. A four-car Class 101 formation is pictured using one of the eight bay platforms that were still connected at that time. The conversion of the North Tyneside Loop and South Shields Branch to Metro operation made most of the bay platform accommodation redundant and only one of the bays remains in use today.

No. 55012 *Crepello* approaches Newcastle Station with the 09.10 from Dundee to London Kings Cross on 13 September 1980. This four-track section was reduced to three tracks after the North Tyneside Loop services were transferred to the Tyne and Wear Metro and diverted underground to a new city centre terminus at St James. No. 55012 was one of the Deltics that received white window surrounds while based at Finsbury Park Depot. It hauled its last train on the night of 13 May 1981, after which it was stripped for spares and officially withdrawn at the end of the month. Its scrapping at Doncaster Works was complete by 18 September.

Facing page: One of several freight-only branches on the south side of the River Tyne served the T.J. Thompson scrapyard at Dunston. No. 31227 propels seven vacuum-braked mineral wagons with scrap from T.J. Thompson and one empty air-braked resin tank from Hexham along the Dunston Branch on 17 July 1986. The train is a trip working from Hexham to Tyne Yard which had to include a brake van because of the mixture of vacuum-braked and air-braked stock – an unusual occurrence at that time because most scrap metal movements had switched to air-braked operation by 1984. The scrap was bound for Lackenby on Teesside and the tank wagon was returning from Hexham to CIBA-Geigy at Duxford near Cambridge.

Facing page: No. 37023 crosses the River Derwent at Derwenthaugh, between Dunston and Blaydon, with a trainload of coal from Swalwell to Stella South on 20 February 1984. This was a journey of less than three miles by rail. Swalwell was a gathering point for lorry-loads of coal from various opencast sites in County Durham, while Stella South was one of a pair of power stations built in the 1950s on opposite banks of the River Tyne. The rail connection to Swalwell was taken out of use in July 1989 and the whole area was redeveloped with retail units and commercial premises. Both the Stella power stations stopped generating electricity in 1991, rail deliveries having finished some years earlier.

No. 31290 passes Derwenthaugh with an eastbound trainload of scrap metal in 21-ton and 16-ton mineral wagons on 20 February 1984. The scrap was from Dunston and the train had just run round at Blaydon before heading back to Tyne Yard. With the train comprising vacuum-fitted wagons the brake van was superfluous on this leg of the journey and did not need to be positioned at the rear. The building in the background belongs to Delta Iron Works, which manufactured iron and steel products for the coal mining industry until 1990. It had once boasted an extensive internal rail system.

Until the early 1980s most passenger trains from the Tyne Valley Line followed the south bank of the Tyne to Blaydon and then crossed the river by means of Scotswood Bridge in order to approach Newcastle on the north bank. A two-car Class 101 unit crosses Scotswood Bridge with the 09.42 from Carlisle to Newcastle on 15 May 1982. The line between Blaydon and Scotswood closed on 4 October 1982 to avoid repairs to the bridge costed at £600,000 and the passenger service was then diverted along the south bank of the Tyne via Derwenthaugh and Dunston. Although the new route was slightly longer, it offered greater opportunities for local traffic and BR later opened two intermediate stations – Dunston in October 1984 and Gateshead Metrocentre in August 1987. Scotswood Bridge remains in place today but carries only pipelines.

The 07.18 from Edinburgh to Carlisle sometimes produced Class 46 haulage and on 31 October 1981 it was the turn of No. 46031 to carry out this duty. The train is pictured near Blaydon. No. 46031 was very much at home in the North East, having been delivered new to Gateshead as No. D168 in May 1962 and remaining based there until its withdrawal in April 1983 apart from a short spell allocated to Leeds Holbeck in 1972.

Having just crossed Scotswood Bridge, No. 47009 rounds the curve towards Blaydon Station with the 07.18 from Edinburgh to Carlisle on 14 November 1981. The signal box is a North Eastern Railway N2 type structure with a 43-lever McKenzie & Holland frame. Passing to the right of the box is the then freight-only line to Gateshead via Dunston, which would become the passenger route to Newcastle just under a year later when the Scotswood Line closed. No. 47009 was delivered new to Finsbury Park as No. D1532 in July 1963 and spent most of its 26-year career based at Eastern Region depots; however at the time of this photograph it was allocated to Haymarket in Edinburgh.

The closure of the Scotswood Line in October 1982 left Blaydon Signal Box with its back to the remaining tracks. Pacer unit No. 143015 has just called at Blaydon with the 10.51 from Hexham to Sunderland on 17 July 1986. All 25 of the Class 143 Pacers were allocated to Heaton Depot when new in 1985-86 and took over from first-generation DMUs on many local services in the North East. The Class 143s later migrated to South Wales and South West England, but accessibility regulations forced their withdrawal and the last examples bowed out in 2021.

Facing page: One of two surviving overhead signal boxes on the Tyne Valley Line, Wylam box was built by the North Eastern Railway in 1897. It gained Grade II listed building status in 1985, by which time its mechanical lever frame had been replaced by a panel. No. 47530 makes a change from the usual diet of Class 101 DMUs as it heads east with an excursion from Dumfries to York on 15 May 1982. No. 47530 was allocated to Crewe Diesel Depot at that time; it later became part of the Network SouthEast fleet, but ended its main-line career working for Rail express systems.

Prudhoe's North Eastern Railway signal box, dating back to 1872, wooden crossing gates and attractive lattice footbridge set the scene for Pacer unit No. 143009 as it arrives with the 10.51 stopper from Hexham to Sunderland on 16 July 1986. Today, Prudhoe retains its signal box and is the most easterly location with semaphore signals on the Tyne Valley Line. The only significant change to the infrastructure at Prudhoe since the 1980s has been the replacement of the wooden gates with lifting barriers.

A four-car Class 101 formation, consisting of cars E56069, E50205, E56396 and E50251, pulls into Hexham Station with a morning train to Carlisle on 28 November 1981. At that time Hexham still offered facilities for freight as well as passengers: the siding next to the train contains seven vacuum-braked vans which had brought animal feeds from South Lynn, and just visible in the distance are a rake of engineer's open wagons and a single tank wagon which had delivered resin from Duxford. Hexham remained an active rail freight location for timber traffic until the late 1990s, but the goods yard site has been redeveloped with retail units.

Facing page: It was not quite the work that they were designed for, but Class 55 Deltics appeared on Tyne Valley passenger workings towards the end of their lives. A visit to Hexham on Saturday 28 November 1981 finds No. 55019 *Royal Highland Fusilier* arriving with the 07.18 Edinburgh to Carlisle service. This was the third appearance of No. 55019 on this working within the month, interspersed between duties on the East Coast Main Line. Just over a month later, on 31 December 1981, No. 55019 was chosen for the last Deltic-hauled scheduled service train, the 16.30 from Aberdeen to York which it worked from Edinburgh.

Facing page: The morning of 28 November 1981 saw a second Deltic pass through Hexham, as No. 55009 *Alycidon* appeared on a circular BR Merrymaker excursion from Newcastle to Carlisle, Edinburgh and back to Newcastle. Although advertised as a Deltic swansong tour, No. 55009 went on to work several further excursions, namely the Grampian Railtour on 12 December, the Deltic Broadsman tour on 19 December, the Trans-Pennine Deltic Lament on 27 December and the Deltic Executive on 29 December. It was chosen as a standby locomotive for the Deltic Farewell railtour on 2 January 1982, but in the event ran only light engine on that date and was then withdrawn from service. The setting here is dominated by Hexham's North Eastern Railway signal box, believed to have been built around 1896 and Grade II listed since 1988. It is still in use today.

Freight traffic on the Tyne Valley Line included occasional block loads of rock salt from Over & Wharton in Cheshire to Hexham freight terminal, where the salt was offloaded for later use on local roads. No. 40158 heads east at Blenkinsop, near Haltwhistle, with 39 wooden-bodied open wagons laden with salt on Saturday 13 February 1982. The locomotive had been reallocated to Carlisle Kingmoor Shed in May 1981, having spent the first twenty years of its career based at Edinburgh Haymarket. It was withdrawn in December 1983 and scrapped at Doncaster Works in 1984. Other freight flows that used the Tyne Valley Line in the early 1980s included oil from Teesport to Carlisle and Dalston, cement from Eastgate to Irvine, bitumen from Ellesmere Port to Elswick, chemicals from Haverton Hill to Stevenston and steel from Lackenby to Workington, as well as some general wagonload and Freightliner traffic. Today, the line carries no freight apart from occasional nuclear flask trains from Hartlepool to Sellafield and railway infrastructure traffic between Carlisle and Tyne Yard.

Facing page: Formerly the junction for the Alston Branch, which closed in 1976, Haltwhistle Station is pictured on 16 July 1984, as a Class 101 unit comprising cars E53246 and E53149 calls with the 10.43 from Carlisle to Newcastle. At that time the 1901-built signal box with its broad timber top mounted on a narrow brick base was still in use. Its signalling functions were transferred to a portable building on the station platform in 1993, but by that time the historic box was Grade II listed, ensuring its survival to the present day. The semaphore signals have long been replaced by colour lights and the track layout has been simplified. The place name Haltwhistle, incidentally, has nothing to do with 'halt' or 'whistle'; its origin is believed to be a combination of two Old English words meaning 'a hill between two streams'.

A Class 101 DMU recedes past Brampton Fell, a few miles over the border in Cumberland, with the 16.52 Carlisle-Newcastle service on 22 July 1985. Brampton Fell Signal Box was built in 1918, its gabled roof being typical for the later years of the North Eastern Railway. The track in the foreground belongs to the up refuge siding which had originally formed a loop controlled at the other end by Hellbeck box; just visible on the far right is the down refuge siding which had also been built as a loop. Today, the refuge sidings have been removed, but the box remains in use as a block post and to control the level crossing.

Standing in for an unavailable DMU, No. 31324 approaches Brampton Station with three Mark I coaches forming the 16.30 from Newcastle to Carlisle on 22 July 1985. The station had been known as Brampton Junction for most of its life until 1971, even though its junction status for passengers had ceased many decades earlier. The short branch from Brampton Junction to Brampton Town had closed to passengers and freight in 1923, while in the opposite direction the line to Tindale Fell never carried a regular passenger service. The whole route between Tindale Fell and Brampton Town had evolved from a late 18th century wagonway built to carry coal and other minerals and finally closed in 1953. A remarkable survivor illustrated here is the shell of Brampton Junction Signal Box, closed in 1966 after the closure of the goods yard but retained for a time thereafter as a permanent way cabin.

Facing page: Class 27 locomotives allocated to Scottish depots occasionally ventured along the Tyne Valley Line on freight workings between Carlisle and Tyne Yard. One such movement is pictured on 22 July 1985, as No. 27055 passes Brampton Fell with a special 11.45 departure from Carlisle. The Class 27 returned from Tyne Yard to Carlisle later in the day to regain familiar territory. No. 27055 was delivered new to the London Midland Region in 1962 but moved to Glasgow Eastfield in 1969 along with other members of the class. It was one of the 24 Class 27s fitted with push-pull equipment for Glasgow-Edinburgh services in the 1970s and renumbered 27109, but returned to the standard fleet as No. 27055 in 1983. It was withdrawn in May 1987.

No. 47069 heads east near Denton School with the 11.45 Stranraer Town to Tyne Yard Speedlink train on 22 July 1985. This working was one of three daily Speedlink wagonload services between Stranraer and North East England operating at that time. The core flow on the outward workings was export steel for Stockton Haulage, but in practice a wide variety of traffic could be carried, some of which joined or left the train at Ayr (Falkland Yard) or Carlisle. On this occasion the payload includes containers from Northern Ireland via Stranraer, empty cement tanks returning from Carlisle to Earles Sidings and empty domestic coal hoppers.

Facing page: The Ponteland Branch closed to passengers in 1929 and the section between Callerton and Ponteland closed completely in 1967, but flows of industrial explosives to ICI Callerton and Rowntrees confectionery to Coxlodge kept the remaining track shiny until the 1980s. Meanwhile, passenger traffic returned when the Tyne and Wear Metro reached a new terminus at Kenton Bank Foot, between Coxlodge and Callerton, in 1981. This meant that BR freight trains ran over Metro infrastructure between Benton and Kenton Bank Foot. No. 31178 propels its short delivery of confectionery from York into the Rowntrees siding on 20 February 1984, having worked the morning trip working from Tyne Yard. The Rowntrees traffic finished in July 1988 and the last train of explosives ran to Callerton in March 1989. The section between Kenton Bank Foot and Callerton was then disused for a short time, but reopened when the Metro was extended to Newcastle Airport in November 1991.

Facing page: The Riverside Branch, which ran close to the north bank of the River Tyne between Byker and Percy Main, lost its passenger service in July 1973 after a long period of decline. It had once formed part of the electrified Tyneside network, which switched to diesel operation in 1967. The line remained open to serve several freight customers after 1973, including the Shepherds scrapyard at St Peters and the Swan Hunter shipyards at Walker and Carville. Deliveries of steel to Swan Hunter declined sharply and the main customer in later years was Shepherds, who sent scrap metal to Sheffield. No. 37078 has just arrived at St Peters with the as-required trip freight from Tyne Yard on 22 July 1985, conveying two wagons for loading. The last recorded working of this train took place on 25 September 1987 and the line was officially taken out of use on 31 March 1988. Today, much of the former trackbed forms part of the popular River Tyne Trail.

Located in the fork of the East Coast Main Line and the suburban line to Tynemouth via Wallsend, Heaton was one of the North Eastern Railway's principal steam sheds, surviving until June 1963 with its own allocation and for two further years as a sub-shed of Gateshead. The site was then redeveloped in the 1970s as a High Speed Train depot, as well as maintaining the local DMU fleet after the closure of South Gosforth Depot. The sidings alongside Heaton Depot were used to stable coaching stock, including the vans which carried newspapers from Manchester to Newcastle each weeknight. No. 40129 snakes out of the sidings with the 13.08 empty vans from Heaton to Manchester Red Bank on 6 December 1981. Today, newspaper trains are a distant memory, but Heaton Depot is still active and has been upgraded to accommodate the latest generation of Intercity Express trains.

Benton Quarry Junction marked the divergence of two curves from the East Coast Main Line, one heading east to the coast via Monkseaton and the other heading west to South Gosforth. The curve towards Monkseaton lost its sparse passenger service in 1978 in readiness for the conversion of the coast line to the Tyne and Wear Metro, but continued to carry freight to and from the Blyth and Tyne network, just as it does today. The curve to South Gosforth lost its main purpose after the closure of South Gosforth DMU depot in 1980, but carried freight to Coxlodge and Callerton until the late 1980s. A High Speed Train set led by power car 43174 joins the main line on 6 December 1981, having been diverted via the Blyth and Tyne because of weekend engineering work. Visible on the left is Benton power signal box, which opened in 1964 and replaced several mechanical boxes both on the main line and on the east-west coast line. The main line between Benton Quarry Junction and Newcastle was electrified twice – first in 1904 for third-rail suburban services, which lasted until 1967, and then in 1991 as part of the East Coast Main Line modernisation programme.

High Speed Trains, later known as InterCity 125 units, were introduced to the East Coast Main Line in 1978 and entered squadron service in the following year. They remained in charge of most London-Edinburgh expresses until the Class 91 electrics arrived in 1991. Even after that, InterCity 125s worked trains that reached beyond the electrified network, such as those to and from Aberdeen. The very last East Coast Main Line service formed by an InterCity 125 took place on 15 December 2019, marking the end of a 41-year period. The photograph shows an Edinburgh-bound train accelerating away from Morpeth on 12 August 1981, while a Class 101 DMU calls at the southbound platform. Just visible on the left is Morpeth Signal Box, which received a new panel in 1991 and is expected to survive until 2056.

Although the Blyth and Tyne network lost its regular passenger services in 1964, the line between Morpeth and Benton via Bedlington provided a useful diversionary route for East Coast expresses when the main line was blocked by engineering work. This option became more attractive in 1980 when BR opened the Hepscott curve at Morpeth, meaning that trains no longer needed to reverse at Morpeth Station. A northbound diversion passes Holywell, north of Backworth, on Sunday 29 November 1981. The Blyth and Tyne Line ceased to be a recognised diversionary route in the late 1980s, but is set to see local passenger trains once again.

Facing page: Holywell Signal Box marked the site of the first Backworth Station, which was originally known as Holywell and handled passengers from 1847 until 1864. An adjacent goods station retained the name Holywell and closed just over a century later in 1965. Meanwhile Backworth's passenger facility was relocated to the Benton-Tynemouth line, where it functioned from 1864 until 1977. Heading south past Holywell on 21 June 1982 is No. 56079 with 27 empty air-braked hopper wagons, likely to have been returning to one of the Durham collieries after delivering coal to Blyth power sation. This stretch of line was singled in January 1985 and Holywell Box was abolished in the following month.

No. 37066 takes the line to Morpeth at Bedlington with a rake of unfitted 21-ton and 24½-ton coal hopper wagons on 21 June 1982. The tracks in the foreground belong to the Ashington Line. The destination of this train is likely to have been Widdrington opencast disposal point, reached by a short branch from the East Coast Main Line about seven miles north of Morpeth. The Bedlington-Morpeth line had been freight-only since 1950 apart from diversions and excursions. Some would like to see the restoration of a regular passenger service between Bedlington and Morpeth as a follow-on scheme to the reopening of the Northumberland line to Ashington. No. 37066 spent the first 25 years of its life working from North East depots and was allocated to Thornaby at the time of this photograph; its last days were spent as a member of the Transrail fleet, working from Wigan Springs Branch until its storage in 1996 and withdrawal in the following year.

Approaching Bedlington Station from the south on 21 June 1982 is No. 56080 with a trainload of coal in air-braked hopper wagons for Blyth power sation. The crossover gives access to Furnaceway Sidings, located just behind the signal box and retained for run-round movements to and from the Morpeth Line. Until 1964 the crossover was also used by northbound passenger trains to enable them to call at Bedlington's single platform. Bedlington South Box is a North Eastern Railway N1 design structure with 30 levers; its opening date is unknown. It originally controlled the access to a local colliery branch as well as the infrastructure that remains in use today.

Facing page: Having headed west with a train of empty hoppers about two hours earlier, No. 37066 comes off the Morpeth Line with a short rake of loaded air-braked hoppers on 21 June 1982. A fully-fitted train such as this did not need a brake van at the rear, but the diagram included workings with unfitted stock for which a brake van had to be provided. The track geometry shows that the first railway through Bedlington was the Morpeth Line, opened as a through route in 1858, while the Ashington Branch – which later became the more important route – opened in stages from 1859 onwards. The 64-lever Bedlington North Signal Box was built in 1912; like its neighbour at the south end of the station it controls a level crossing as well as points and signals. The small gantry controlling the divergence of lines to Morpeth and Ashington was later replaced by a bracket signal on the west side of the line.

The Cambois Branch, serving North Blyth, opened in 1867 and originally diverged from the Bedlington-Ashington line by means of a south-facing junction at West Sleekburn. A new curve was laid between Marchey's House Junction and Winning in 1893, creating a triangle of lines and enabling direct movements between Ashington and Cambois. Winning Signal Box dates back to 1895, but its original frame was replaced by a smaller one in 1963. No. 37048 is signalled to take the northern curve from Winning to Marchey's House Junction with a trainload of imported alumina from North Blyth to Lynemouth on 17 July 1986. Today there are no longer any scheduled trains via the northern curve, but it remains part of the network. The bracket signal was replaced by a pair of modern steel posts, still with semaphore arms, in the early 21st century.

The short-distance flow of imported alumina from North Blyth to Lynemouth benefited from a new generation of air-braked rolling stock in the early 1990s. Carrying the obsolete BR Trainload Petroleum livery, No. 37893 approaches Freeman's Crossing on the Cambois Branch with empty air-braked tanks returning to North Blyth on 21 February 1995. At that time BR's bulk freight operations had recently been divided between three pre-privatisation divisions and this flow was operated by Transrail, despite being wholly within Loadhaul territory. That was because the traffic dovetailed with Transrail's longer-distance alumina flow from North Blyth to Fort William, which was allocated to Transrail because it terminated in Scotland. No. 37893 was formerly No. 37177 and received its new identity after refurbishment and modification for heavy freight work in 1987. It worked infrastructure trains in Italy from 2001 until 2003 and went into storage soon after its return to Britain, although its official withdrawal did not take place until 2009.

The Cambois Branch served numerous customers, but by the 1990s its business was dominated by two flows: coal to Cambois 'A' and 'B' power stations and alumina from North Blyth. The power station traffic switched from manual-discharge hoppers to merry-go-round stock in the 1980s, which helped to make the operation more efficient. A busy moment is captured at Freeman's Crossing on 21 February 1995, as No. 56065 waits to take the short power station branch with the 08.46 departure from Wardley while sister locomotive No. 56091 takes charge of the 11.45 empties from Cambois to Tyne Yard. Both locomotives are still in existence today: No. 56065 was rebuilt for GB Railfreight as No. 69009, while No. 56091 works for DC Rail. Cambois 'A' and 'B' power stations closed in 1999 and 2001 respectively. The Cambois Branch began carrying coal in the opposite direction when a loading terminal opened at Battleship Wharf in 2006; this traffic finished in 2021.

No. 37067 nears the end of its journey to West Blyth staiths on 6 March 1982 with a train of shipment coal in unfitted and vacuum-braked hopper wagons. On the right is Cambois diesel depot, which opened in 1968 to replace steam sheds at North Blyth, South Blyth and Percy Main. Cambois did not have its own allocation of main-line locomotives but was the day-to-day base for the traction used on the Blyth and Tyne system. This consisted mainly of Class 37s, giving way to Class 56s in the 1980s. The need for a depot at Cambois diminished in line with the gradual decline in the freight business and the depot closed in 1994 in favour of a centralised facility at Tyne Yard. The demolition of Cambois Depot began in 2006 and the site has since been completely cleared.

The North Eastern Railway was well known for building raised wooden staiths from which hopper wagons could discharge their coal into waiting ships. Several examples were located along the coast of Northumberland and County Durham, and one of the biggest installations was at West Blyth. No. 37065 runs round its train at West Blyth on 6 March 1982 after forming an inward working from one of the North East pits. The operation later switched to using air-braked merry-go-round hoppers, but tonnages declined and the staiths closed altogether in 1989. A similar facility at Bates, on the opposite side of the River Blyth, had ceased operating in 1984.

Located right at the end of the Cambois Branch, North Blyth alumina import terminal opened in 1970 to supply the Alcan smelter at Lynemouth, a distance of about eight miles by rail. The alumina was shipped to North Blyth from Scandinavia and, later, from Limerick in the Republic of Ireland. Because the flow covered such a short distance and used freight-only tracks, the customer provided a fleet of covered hopper wagons with no continuous brake, usually referred to as unfitted stock. These wagons were the last unfitted vehicles to be built for the BR network. No. 37048 sets back under the loader with empty hoppers from Lynemouth on 17 July 1986. The North Blyth-Lynemouth flow came to an end in 2012 when Lynemouth smelter closed, but the import terminal is still used today to load alumina for Fort William, which is now the last remaining freight flow on the Cambois Branch.

Facing page: The first railway to reach Ashington was a mineral branch from the East Coast Main Line, but in 1872 the Blyth and Tyne Railway opened its line from North Seaton to Newbiggin-on-Sea and this line became the principal railway route through Ashington. A junction just north of Ashington Station gave access to Ashington Colliery and the mineral branch from the East Coast Main Line, as well as a separate mineral branch to Linton and Butterwell. No. 37069 negotiates that junction as it approaches Ashington Station with a trainload of coal from Ashington colliery on 21 June 1982. Today there is no longer a junction at this location and the remaining tracks carry only biomass to Lynemouth; the new Ashington Station is a single-platform terminus located on the west side of the line just behind the photographer.

Facing page: Ashington Colliery was an extraordinary relic in the late 20th century, with an extensive rail system that was used both by BR coal trains and by National Coal Board (NCB) trains carrying coal and shale. The NCB traction included a fleet of former BR Class 14 diesel-hydraulic locomotives, which had only worked for BR for a few years before being declared redundant because of reductions in local freight traffic. In total Ashington was host to 19 Class 14s for varying lengths of time between 1968 and 1987. NCB No. 31, formerly BR No. D9531, arrives at Ashington with a mixture of ex-BR and internal hopper wagons on 17 July 1986. This locomotive had worked for BR from January 1965 until December 1967; it was then sold for scrap but purchased by the NCB in 1968 for use at various collieries, taking up residence at Ashington in 1974. After the Ashington system closed in 1986, No. 31 was again sold for scrap, but this time it was saved for preservation by a team from the East Lancashire Railway.

Outliving most other mines in the once thriving Northumberland Coalfield, Ashington produced coal from 1867 until October 1986. The town of Ashington owes its existence to this and other nearby collieries, with over 5,000 miners living and working there when the industry was in full swing. Rail transport played an essential part in the distribution of coal to ports, power stations and other consumers. Three different wagon types are in evidence in the yard on 17 July 1986: No. 37084 sets out with loaded vacuum-braked hoppers, while the sidings also contain BR merry-go-round hoppers and NCB wooden-bodied stock. Visible on the right are the NCB workshops, which remained active until the colliery closed.

Facing page: Headed by NCB No. 1, formerly BR Class 14 No. D9500, a train of empty NCB hoppers including some ex-BR vehicles takes the curve from Ashington Loop towards Ashington Colliery on 17 July 1986. No. D9500 was the prototype of the Class 14s, having emerged from Swindon Works in July 1964. It worked in South Wales and in the Bristol area until its withdrawal from BR stock in April 1969. It was then purchased by the NCB and based at Ashington until 1986. Since then the locomotive has been stationed on various preserved railways and museum sites including the Llangollen Railway, Swindon, West Somerset Railway, Meadowhall, Barrow Hill and Peak Rail, but without ever being restored to working order. Overall, the Class 14s have fared well in preservation, with 19 of the original 56 locomotives still extant.

The main line beyond Ashington originally ran via Woodhorn to Newbiggin-on-Sea. The section between Woodhorn and Newbiggin-on-Sea closed to all traffic in 1964, but a branch from Woodhorn to Lynemouth had been built in the 1950s and this branch provided rail access to the Alcan smelter when it opened in the early 1970s. The smelter generated outgoing trains of aluminium slab as well as receiving alumina from North Blyth. No. 37048 passes the former Woodhorn Colliery with a trainload of alumina for Lynemouth on 17 July 1986. Coal was brought to the surface at Woodhorn from 1894 until 1981; today the site lives on as a museum, offering insights into the industry that dominated this part of the country for most of the 20th century.

While Northumberland's deep mines closed one by one, opencast activity sometimes provided new opportunities. A rapid loading bunker for opencast coal was commissioned at Butterwell in 1977, reached by a short spur from the East Coast Main Line as well as by a branch from the NCB line that once ran from Ashington to Linton and Longhirst mines. The route from Ashington was unusual in being controlled by the NCB but used exclusively by BR trains. A visit to Butterwell on 17 July 1986 finds No. 56080 in charge of a typical merry-go-round working, which had arrived via Ashington but would depart after loading via the East Coast Main Line. The Ashington route passed into BR ownership in 1987 but became unusable in the 1990s because of repeated vandalism. Trains continued to run to and from Butterwell – and latterly to and from a nearby site at Potland Burn – via the East Coast Main Line spur until 2015.